Panda

A DAVID & CHARLES BOOK
© F&W Media International, Ltd 2008, 2012

David & Charles is an imprint of F&W Media
International, Ltd
Brunel House, Forde Close, Newton
Abbot, TQ12 4PU, UK

F&W Media International, Ltd is a subsidiary of
F+W Media, Inc
10151 Carver Road, Suite #200,
Blue Ash, OH 45242, USA

Text and illustrations © Heather Angel 2008, 2012

First published in the UK and USA in 2008
This paperback edition first
published in the UK in 2012

A catalogue record for this book is
available from the British Library.

ISBN-13: 978-1-4463-0286-6 paperback
ISBN-10: 1-4463-0286-5 paperback

Printed in Singapore by KHL Printing Co.Pte Ltd for:
F&W Media International, Ltd
Brunel House, Forde Close, Newton
Abbot, TQ12 4PU, UK

10 9 8 7 6 5 4 3 2 1

Commissioning Editor: Neil Baber
Editor: Emily Pitcher
Desk Editor: Demelza Hookway
Project Editor: Caroline Taggart
Design Manager: Sarah Clark
Production Manager: Beverley Richardson

F+W Media publishes high quality books on a wide
range of subjects.
For more great book ideas visit: www.fwmedia.co.uk

Panda

An intimate portrait of one of the
world's most elusive animals

Heather Angel

D&C
David and Charles

Contents

Introduction

The giant panda oozes charm and charisma and is loved the world over. Who could fail to be captivated by this uniquely endearing animal, with its large, friendly face and eyes that are exaggerated by black eye patches? Confined to China, it is far and away the country's most famous animal. Not surprisingly, it is regarded as a national treasure, known as *daxiong mao*, meaning 'large cat bear'. Yet it is now so rare that very few people have seen one in the wild.

The panda has achieved iconic status and in captivity it is frequently given a repetitive name as a mark of respect. Chi Chi – who lived at London Zoo for 14 years in the 1960s and 1970s – inspired the logo, designed by Peter Scott, for the newly formed World Wildlife Fund; and Jing Jing, born in Chengdu Research Base for Giant Panda Breeding on 30 August 2006, is the mascot for the 2008 Beijing Olympic Games.

Biologically, the panda is something of an anomaly; it has the dentition and gut of a carnivore, yet it is a vegetarian feeding almost exclusively on bamboo. We know from fossil remains that pandas once lived as far south as northern Vietnam and Myanmar and as far north as Beijing, but climate change and forest destruction pushed them northwards to the eastern edge of the Tibetan plateau in their quest for life-giving bamboo groves. Road construction further fragmented their forest home and today pandas are confined to a few mountain reserves in three provinces – Sichuan, Shaanxi and Gansu.

In recent years, much time and money have been invested in panda conservation to help halt the decline in numbers. In 1998, a logging ban was enforced in all panda reserves, and some farmlands have been reforested. Fragmented reserves have been linked by the planting of bamboo corridors, which help pandas to find new food sources when all their favoured bamboo in an area dies off after simultaneous flowering. The corridors also serve to extend the gene pool, enabling the pandas to move further from their home territories and mate with unrelated individuals.

When the Third National Panda Survey was undertaken in 2004, more sophisticated survey methods resulted in an upwards revision of the estimated total wild population from 1,000 to 1,590 individuals. There are now 40 panda reserves, compared with only 13 two decades ago.

Early attempts to breed pandas in captivity were very hit and miss, but now the success rate is high, with more cubs being born each year and the total number of captive pandas exceeding 180. Sadly, however, the first attempt to introduce a captive-bred panda into the wild was short-lived. A five-year-old male named Xiang Xiang was released from the China Conservation and Research Center for the Giant Panda at Wolong in April 2006, having been trained for almost three years in all the necessary skills needed to survive in the wild, and fitted with a radio collar to enable conservationists to track his movements. Less than a year later, his body was found on the snow. From the extensive damage to one side of the body, it is thought that he may have fallen from some height after a fight with another male panda.

Researchers will build on this experience, and the project to release captive-bred pandas into the wild will continue. Pandas will be given better survival training and next time a female may be selected in preference to a male. Another possibility is that several animals could be set free in an area that once had a natural panda population.

Although the giant panda is instantly recognizable, a book on pandas would be incomplete without devoting a chapter to its lesser-known red cousin. Despite its name, this appealing animal is more closely related to the raccoon, but shares some of the giant panda's bear-like characteristics and habits.

The images in this book have been selected from literally thousands taken during seven trips to China over a period of 13 years, specifically to photograph pandas in different seasons. Perhaps the most memorable trip was when I climbed, together with my guide, porter and cook, to the huts where Dr George Schaller, the distinguished American zoologist, worked with other scientists, researching pandas 2,530 metres (8,300 feet) up at Wuyipeng. As I rounded the last corner I saw dagger-like icicles hanging from the roofs. There was no heating in my hut and the bedding was damp. I slept with all my clothes on, but this meant I had a speedy rise at first light to see the forest blanketed with fresh snow. As I walked along the narrow tracks I heard the haunting call of a tragopan pheasant. It was an unforgettable moment.

Why do I keep returning to photograph the panda? Quite simply because it is my favourite animal. I hope that *Panda* will give others an insight into why it has become a flagship species in the world of conservation. Let us trust that it is not too late to save this very special animal – for life on earth would be the poorer without it.

Panda Places

Confined to a few mountain ranges on the east of the Tibetan Plateau, giant pandas amble through forests often bathed in mist, seeking bamboo groves. On their way, they wander past towering rhododendrons ablaze with spring flowers or trees glowing in vibrant autumn livery. Between feeding sessions, they may take a drink or a nap while youngsters play. This chapter gives an insight into some of the striking natural features within the panda's favoured haunts – portrayed here in different seasons.

Misty Mountains ▷

Often during the summer, mist swirls around
the conifer-clad peaks and through the valleys
of the Qionglai Mountains, creating a scene
reminiscent of a Chinese painting. This,
together with abundant rain and snow, helps
to maintain the moist atmosphere which is
essential if bamboos are to flourish.

◄ **A Mountain Backdrop**
A panda sits on a rock to feed on a fine spring day with the hazy mountain backdrop behind. The Qionglai Mountains contain the largest area where wild giant pandas live and some 40 per cent of the total population occurs here.

Relaxing in Spring ▷
A panda sits comfortably against one branch of a tree fork, warming itself in the first rays of the early morning sun after a cool night.

◁ A Spring Kaleidoscope

For a few brief days in spring, as the buds break on the deciduous trees bordering the Pitiao River at Wolong Panda Reserve, the forests become a patchwork of colours more typical of autumn. This ephemeral kaleidoscope of acid yellows, bronzes and pale greens gradually changes to a uniform dull green as the leaves open out and the green chlorophyll pigment develops.

▽ Rhododendron Flowers

At the same time as the leaves appear on the deciduous trees, rhododendrons burst into flower, decorating the forest hillsides with patches of pink and white where bees home in to forage on the blooms.

Keeping a Low Profile ▷
The profile of the giant panda's large head is much reduced as it lies relaxing on the ground with its face turned to one side and partially hidden in the grass.

▽ **Golden Monkey Mother and Baby**
The snub-nosed golden monkey shares the giant panda's habitat and can be found living in troops at both Jiuzhaigou and Wolong. As a troop moves through the forest, foraging on plants and fruits, and the monkeys leap from one tree to another, their glowing golden coats enliven the drabbest of scenes. Their faces look as though they have been made up with blue eye shadow and outsized white lips, with the small upturned nose squeezed in between them. Here, a pale golden baby nestles tightly against its mother's deep golden pelt.

▲ **Autumn in Jiuzhaigou**
North-east of Wolong lies Jiuzhaigou, or Nine Village Valley, with an amazing series of colourful lakes and cascading waterfalls. This magical valley was unknown to the outside world until a team of foresters visited it in 1975. Jiuzhaigou's sheer beauty and rich biodiversity led to its being declared a World Heritage Site in 1992. Now it has become a top tourist venue, with 1.5 million visitors a year travelling up the valley in eco-friendly buses decorated with pictures of pandas. Many rare animals, including giant and red pandas, inhabit the Jiuzhaigou forests.

Winter In Wolong

Winter may lack colourful spring flowers and autumn foliage, but it has a special beauty of its own, with more open vistas through the leafless trees. When rhododendrons are in flower their leaves pass unnoticed, but come winter they exhibit graphic shapes silhouetted against a misty backdrop. Perennially green bamboo is also transformed by a dusting of snow. Indeed, Ruth Harkness, the American who brought the first live giant panda back to the western world in 1936, remarks in her account of her expedition that she had never seen a stranger thing than snow on green bamboo. In the picture on the far right, a panda pauses beside the Pitiao River with the snowy mountain backdrop visible behind.

Waterfall in Spring ▶

A small waterfall flows down a rock face into the Pitiao River. This is taken from the same view as the winter shot on page 100. After heavy rain, the increased water flow widens the narrow fall and a walk through the dense forest is enlivened by the sound of falling water interspersed with wildlife chirpings and calls.

◄ **Resting amongst Ferns**
The large white head appears almost to glow from amongst the lush fern blanket which encircles and hides the rest of the panda's body.

▲ **Plant Hunter's Delight**
One of the joys of visiting panda country in spring is seeking out an array of attractive wild flowers – often in quite unexpected places. I found this *Daiswa polyphylla* quite by chance as I placed my photo pack on the ground beside it.

◄ ◄ **A Riverine Scene**
A panda feeds, then rests a while beside a rippling river fed by smaller streams and waterfalls, such as the one cascading down the hill behind. Eventually it gets up by rolling over on to one side and pushing up with one hind leg and one front paw.

A Forest Ravine ▷
The problems that both researchers and
rangers face – whether searching for pandas
or for potential poachers – are apparent from
this shot. The hillsides are not only
covered by thick forest, but they are also
punctuated by deep ravines which make for
slow progress along narrow or even
non-existent paths.

Up in a Fork ▷

A seven-month-old panda cub plays on its own in the fork of a tree. Youngsters with their smaller bodies do not have to spend as much time feeding as adults and so can devote time each day to playing.

◄ ► **Playing in a Pine Tree**
Seen from a distance, this young panda at first appears as little more than a small speck amongst the dense coniferous branches. However, a longer lens reveals how it uses the branches close to the trunk to perfect its climbing technique through play.

◄ Spring on Emei Shan

Mount Omei or Emei Shan (*shan* means mountain) is the most famous of four sacred Buddhist mountains in China. It is also a plant hunter's and bird watcher's paradise, with tree-like rhododendrons, magnolias and many important medicinal plants. Giant pandas roamed here as recently as 1948.

In the Pink ►

A pensive young panda sits alone in a clearing amongst pink wild flowers in early summer. Moments later it was up and wandering along a path before frolicking down a slope. The swift change in behavioural pattern is typical of young animals.

Riverside View

As the snow meltwaters drop, the Pitiao River flows past forest that in places virtually touches the water. Elsewhere, inaccessible sheer rock faces border the river on one side, with an exposed pebble and sand beach below a green bank on the other. Here a panda sits on the bank beside the fast-flowing river in the spring.

◄ ◄ Mother and Baby

Pandas sometimes give birth to twins, but in the wild a mother rarely raises both cubs. Males play no part in rearing the young – after mating both adults return to their solitary ways. At birth, a panda cub is a squirming pink, rat-like animal with an obvious tail. This four-month-old, captive-bred cub is still feeding on its mother's milk and is clearly very dependent on her.

Chilling Out ►

In the past, China gave away pandas to other countries as prized diplomatic gifts or as short-term loans to zoos. Nowadays, because of concerns over the possible health risks of long-haul flights, the only way that a foreign zoo can exhibit a giant panda is under the rent-a-panda scheme, whereby they rent the animals from China for a ten-year-period. All cubs born abroad belong to China. Washington National Zoo has two adult pandas housed in spacious enclosures which can be viewed during Washington daylight hours on pandacams. Here, one of the pandas is chilling out on a warm day in an air-conditioned cave.

A Bamboo Diet

Pandas are the most vegetarian of all bears, with bamboo making up 99 per cent of all they eat. Yet they have not always had such a monotonous diet; panda ancestors were carnivores and modern-day pandas retain a carnivorous gut. Over time their diet changed, but they have not completely lost their appetite for meat. Today, they may no longer have the body or the metabolism to hunt active prey, but they will still eat any carrion they come across.

Forest Bamboos
The lower level of the mixed forest at Wolong includes both evergreen bamboos and deciduous trees which leaf out during late spring. Here, on the banks of the Pitiao River, the tips of bamboo stems bend down to touch the water's edge.

Managing Bamboo ▷
Bamboos are outsized grasses with woody stems known as culms. When a panda starts to feed on a large leafy culm, it has to cope with leaves flopping down over its face. Once the side branches have been bitten off and a bunch of leaves gathered at the side of the mouth, the stem can either be held in a paw to one side of the face or discarded.

Bamboo Feeding Ritual

Before a panda eats bamboo leaves it has to process them. Firstly, the side shoots are bitten off the stem and rolled into a bunch with the tongue, so that the tips of the shoots project from one side of the mouth. Then, once a sizeable leafy bunch has accumulated, the panda holds it with a paw so that manageable portions can be bitten from the cut ends.
In winter, bamboo may be eaten with snow still remaining on the leaves.

Powerful Jaws and Teeth

The panda's appealing large head contains powerful jaw muscles which – together with the enlarged cheek teeth with bear tubercles to help with grinding – play an essential part in crushing the tough bamboo stems. A stem is fed in at right angles to the corner of the mouth. At the same time as the panda bites the stem, the paw is jerked up and down to help break it. The open mouth reveals the powerful incisor teeth.

Remains of a Feast

When feeding on large bamboo shoots, pandas use their
incisor teeth to rip the tough outer covering, which is removed as
the paw and head are moved away from each other. With a ready
supply of food nearby, a panda soon ends up with a pile of bamboo
debris on its belly.

Foraging in Ferns

A panda often adopts a relaxed reclining position for feeding: then only the arm and jaw muscles need to work in harmony in order to process enough bamboo. During a 24-hour period a panda consumes from 12–30kg (26–84lb) of bamboo – the amount varies with the season and the condition of the leaves and stems. This one is starting to feed on a bamboo shoot just after a carpet of ferns has produced new fronds in spring.

A Huge Head

Only when a panda looks skywards can the massive breadth of the head be fully appreciated. This angle shows how the erect black ears repeat the colour of the eye patches. A panda's skin is not uniform in colour: the black fur arises from black pigmented areas, while the white fur lies above pink skin.

Panda Paws

Bears' paws are generally well adapted for holding food and other objects, for grasping tree trunks and for digging and scratching. But a panda's forepaws are specially adapted for manipulating bamboo stems, with a modified elongated wrist bone forming the pseudothumb covered by a fleshy pad. Instead of bending down to feed on bamboo stems *in situ*, this allows the panda to bite off a stem which it then grasps and manipulates by wedging it between the base of the forepaw digits and the pseudothumb.

Bamboo-eating Bear

Bamboos will grow for decades, but periodically all the plants in an area will flower simultaneously and then die. When this happens, pandas can literally starve to death if they cannot find a new bamboo patch. In the past, when the bamboo belts were much more extensive and continuous than they are today, this was not usually a problem, but in the 1970s bamboo die-off in Wolong resulted in the deaths of several pandas. Now, an important part of panda conservation work is the planting of bamboos to create corridors that link the fragmented reserves.

All-weather Pandas

Regardless of the weather, pandas have to feed on bamboo for up to 14 hours in every 24, both during the day and into the night. Come sun, rain or snow, this is done for 20–25 years in the wild and even longer in captivity.

Wrestling with Bamboo

Whether propped up against a tree trunk or lying on the ground, a six-month-old cub has to begin to get to grips with leafy bamboo stems. Holding a stem in a paw, it looks up at the leaves, then experiments, using all four limbs to wrestle with the grass it will depend on for the rest of its life.

A Monotonous Diet

Other large herbivores such as antelopes graze on grass every day, but their extra-large stomachs allow the food to ferment when it is further broken down by gut microbes. This ensures more efficient digestion, as the cell walls are also broken down. However, the panda's short gut – a relic of its carnivorous past – lacks microbes and digests little more than the cell content, which is why it has to spend so much time eating in order to gain the nourishment it needs to survive in its harsh mountainous habitat.

A Panda Dropping

The highly fibrous dropping passed by a panda shows just how poorly the bamboo leaves are digested. Indeed, it is estimated that a panda digests only some 12–25 per cent of the food it eats. Bamboo has long been utilized for making many different products in China, from cooking utensils and pushchairs to ladders, rafts and scaffolding; now someone has hit on a novel way of making money from the droppings of captive pandas by converting the shredded bamboo into odour-free souvenirs such as photo frames and bookmarks.

On the Move

Pandas have to move to find food and to drink, but the sheer size and weight of an adult giant panda means that for most of its life it ambles along at a leisurely speed, conserving precious energy. Panda cubs, on the other hand, have plenty of surplus vitality and enjoy climbing trees or rolling on the ground – especially when a snowfall provides a soft carpet to cushion their fall.

Following a Path

Many of the trails which pandas use on a regular basis are along well-worn paths, but by late spring creepers begin to grow quickly and can encroach on a track. In this case the panda is walking low beneath a robust creeper in the rain. Also, in stormy weather, broken branches can fall across paths, creating a potential hazard.

Striding Out

Like other bears, a panda walks with head held down below the shoulders, with the result that the jaws come close to touching a front foot that is raised when walking. The sharp claws and strong teeth are powerful weapons that a panda can use to defend itself against predators, such as a solitary clouded leopard or a pack of dhole (red dogs), which will attack young pandas or decrepit, old individuals.

A Pigeon-toed Gait

Only when you see a giant panda walking towards you can you appreciate the pigeon-toed gait. This is most obvious on a young animal, before the limbs are fully grown and the leg muscles well developed.

A panda's body is not designed for speed, but it can trot for short bursts if need be to escape from a rival. It can also climb a tree to avoid a dhole attack.

Climbing a Tree

Some pandas – especially younger ones – enjoy climbing trees more than others. Before it starts to climb, a panda pulls itself upright on to its hind legs, holding on to the trunk with one or both forepaws. After pushing off from the ground, it grasps the trunk with its powerful forearms to pull itself up. As the hind feet move up, the panda can stretch out alternate arms to help its progress. On the way, side branches may have to be navigated.

Taking a Drink

After feeding, a panda likes to drink. This is done quite silently: instead of lapping like a cat, the panda brings its lips close down to the water so it can suck it up. Here the panda's head is reflected in the calm water. After drinking from a small pool, it backs away before walking off for a rest and yet another feed.

A Riverside Walk
At first pondering a safe place to step, a panda eventually picks out a route across an exposed boulder beach bordering the Pitiao River. It walks with care from one rock to another, at one stage climbing up on to a large rock, to avoid slipping into the cold winter water.

◄ A Forest Encounter

For most of their life, giant pandas live a solitary existence, only rarely meeting up with others of their species. When a female is on heat, she homes in on a male by detecting his scent and by scent-marking more frequently herself. Pandas are at their most vocal when courting, exchanging a variety of mating calls such as barks, bleats, chirps and moans.

Checking out a Scent Mark ►

A panda sniffs at the ground to check the scent left by another panda. Giant pandas have an acute sense of smell which helps to compensate for their poor eyesight.

Camouflage

As a panda moves through a green or brown forest interior, the black and white body completely fails to blend in with the surroundings. Come the winter, it merges in remarkably well with the dark trunks and white snow – especially when glimpsed walking through a forest as a small part of the overall scene. It is difficult to explain the significance of a colouration that appears to benefit an animal for only part of the year.

Getting off the Ground
A panda cub stands up against a trunk to decide the best approach to climbing it. Hugging the trunk with its forepaws, it can lift one foot off the ground as the other pushes off. These back views of a cub show how the black stripe running across the shoulders forms a continuous black band with the forelegs.

◀ Scaling a Tree

Climbing a conifer with a bare lower trunk seems straightforward at first. But things become more difficult when the panda reaches the drooping evergreen branches and has to spend time weaving its way through them.

Beginning to Descend
A panda can descend a tree either forwards or backwards. Going down head first enables it to see and negotiate any obstacles in its path.

A Rapid Descent ▷
Hugging the trunk with its arms and also gripping with its hind feet, a panda descends feet first like a fireman down a pole. If it should misjudge the landing, it can rely on its thick, oily coat to cushion the fall.

Playful Pandas

Typical of young mammals, panda cubs love to play – with each other or with anything they can get their paws on. Any natural object they come across, whether it be bamboo stems, pieces of bark, twigs, leaves or stones, is picked up, played with and discarded. As their climbing skills increase, so they venture higher up trees. If a mother manages to raise twins, this is a bonus, since both then have a playmate.

Hide-and-Seek
The swift-changing mood of a young panda is illustrated by two shots taken within a few minutes of each other. One moment this ten-month-old cub was sitting soulfully on a fallen branch, then it moved along and began to peek through some cascading branches to play hide-and-seek.

A Novel Game
After climbing up on to a forked branch, a six-month-old panda cub grasps an upper branch with its forepaws, so that it can dance on the lower one.

Gymnastics

A six-month-old youngster makes its way along the underside of a horizontal log by clinging on with its arms and one leg, and moving one arm forward at a time. Then it loses its balance, but prevents itself from falling by gripping on with both forepaws, swinging precariously from side to side in the process.

A Playful Wrestle

Like young mammals the world over, panda cubs enjoy spending time play-wrestling either by boxing each other with a paw or rolling over on the ground interlocked. Play is an important part of young pandas' development as they learn new skills which will help them to look after themselves later in life.

Acrobatic Skills ▷

Once a feeding session is over, young pandas revert to playful activities, which often include climbing. A side branch on a dead tree makes a convenient back rest as a panda cub sits in the fork, propping itself up with a paw on the tree trunk.

◄ Taking it Easy

Finding a comfortable support is everything. This completely relaxed cub is hunkered down in the fork of a tree, with one paw ready to steady its body should it begin to slip.

Antics in a Tree
When a panda does not want to see something, it uses one or both paws to cover its eyes.
For such a bulky animal it is surprising how well a panda manoeuvres itself – albeit slowly
– up in a tree. Starting from an upright position, it twists and turns its body until it is horizontal.
Then it continues to turn so that it is effectively doing a headstand and begins to move down the tree.

A Playful Slide

While these two pandas were playing together on the edge of a bank, the lower of the two lost its balance and began to slide down the slope; still locked together it carried the other panda with it.

◄ ▼ Clasping a Tree

In the picture on the left, an immature panda has made its way up between two parallel branches so that it can rest its body against one whilst grasping the other with its forepaws. Below, an older, more experienced animal has found a safer place to rest perched on a side branch, so that it only has to rest one paw lightly on another branch. Occasionally, a panda misjudges the strength of a bough and ends up crashing to the ground, but its thick coat softens the fall, so it soon rights itself and ambles off.

Gaining a Clear View ▷
If a branch is in the way, a panda will
turn its head to get an unobstructed
view beneath or to one side of a
branch in preference to moving its
body – especially if it is tightly wedged
in position in the tree.

A Relaxing Roll

Young pandas, in particular, love to somersault and they will do this repeatedly as they play on the ground or with another cub. Even when not somersaulting, they move their legs and arms incessantly in all directions as they roll back and forth.

Playing with Bamboo

For a young panda, a bamboo stem makes a fun object to play with. Whether using the front paws on their own or in conjunction with the hind paws, the cub manipulates the bamboo in ways which can be useful when it needs to hold on to a stem to feed on the leaves.

Hugging a Tree ▷
Stepping up to a tree trunk, a young panda hugs it with its arms and looks around the side. Such large trees are difficult for young pandas to climb because they cannot reach far enough around the trunk to gain a secure grip. For this reason, they prefer saplings and smaller trees.

◀ **A Tête-à-Tête**

Two panda cubs playing in the same tree nuzzle
up to each other in a friendly meeting. At this
stage, pandas display a camaraderie that is lost
as they mature and stake out their territories.

Pandas in Winter

The panda's mountain habitat is transformed in winter,
when snow falls and blankets the ground for several months.
Although pandas are well adapted for survival in these conditions,
they will descend to lower, slightly warmer levels during the
coldest period. Come the warmer spring days the pandas then
migrate up the mountains again. In this way, they can exploit
different bamboo glades.

◄◄ A Winter Wonderland

Wolong Reserve lies in the Qionglai Mountains, where a mixed forest clothing the lower slopes gives way to coniferous forest above. As winter progresses, the snowline moves down the mountains, maintaining a white mantle for several months. At the lowest levels snow is more ephemeral, melting during the day from the warmth of the winter sun.

◄ Frozen Waterfall

In winter at Wolong, small waterfalls freeze to become ice falls. When it snows, as here, the whole forest becomes an enchanting wilderness as snow etches the branching patterns of deciduous trees and carpets the dead herb layer.

Winter Feast ▷

Sitting on the snow, a panda does what it does every day – feeds on bamboo. The green leaves add a small patch of colour to this monochromatic image on an overcast day following an overnight snowfall.

Subsnow Stream
Within the panda's mountain habitat, streams continue to flow, even after repeated snowfalls. Together with springs, these freely flowing streams provide accessible water sources for pandas to drink throughout the winter. On a quiet winter's morning the sound of a babbling brook is often heard before it is seen.

Pausing to Reflect
Walking across exposed rocks beside the Pitiao River at Wolong, a panda pauses with its body reflected in a calm backwater. Pandas have been seen swimming across rivers, but they are by no means avid swimmers.

An Elevated Viewpoint

Pandas begin to climb trees when they are just six months old. Youngsters climb for the fun of it and also to escape from predators, whereas adults save energy by keeping to flattish ground. A bare winter tree with a solid fork provides a secure vantage point from which to survey the surrounding forest blanketed by an overnight snowfall. It is also a great place for a lone cub to frolic.

Abstract Rhododendrons ▲

The Wolong Reserve is a highly biodiverse habitat with a wonderful array of wild flowers and flowering shrubs as well as trees. Many different kinds of rhododendron flower in spring. The branching pattern of larger specimens becomes more obvious in winter, when the evergreen leaves roll up and hang down, an adaptation to help them combat the cold.

Rhododendron Leaves and Pine Needles ▷

After a cold night, the tightly rolled and drooping rhododendron leaves look quite different from their normal broad shape. As the temperature gradually rises during the day, the leaves open and slowly rise towards their normal horizontal position. But with the short winter days the cold can set in before the leaves are completely flat. This study of leaves growing adjacent to pine needles is reminiscent of a Chinese ink-brush painting.

◀ ▲ Snow Roll
Like any young animals adapted to survive outside in snowy conditions, panda cubs enjoy a winter frolic, repeatedly rolling over on the soft ground.

Panda Slide
A nonchalant stroll up a slope suddenly turns into a nightmare descent for a panda. Losing its balance on a snowy slope, it slithers unceremoniously on its back, head downwards, with all four limbs up in the air. Tracks found by researchers in deep snow show that a panda will toboggan down a slope on its belly, apparently for fun.

Lounging

Pandas – young and old – are great loungers, but most especially the adults. They spend so much time eating that they need to rest whenever possible to help conserve the energy required to forage and feed. Rocks, banks, tree trunks, branches and even snow drifts are all utilized to prop them up when feeding or simply to pause a while and rest. The thick pelt helps to soften any rough edges, although the emergent rocks in the Pitiao River tend to be well rounded.

Climbing a Tree

A young panda uses a hind leg to gain lift before climbing a sapling. The front limbs hug the trunk and, once the panda is off the ground, the claws on all four limbs help it to gain a firm grip on the bark. Trees with bare lower trunks are easier to climb and are favoured over coniferous trees with drooping branches. As the panda climbs and shakes the branches, it is showered with falling snow.

Reclining on Snow to Feed

A snow bank makes a soft, cushioned back rest for a reclining panda as it feeds during winter. The stiff, coarse pelt is also oily, which provides excellent insulation against the cold and wet. The snowy coating on the black arms is proof of how little heat the animal loses through its thick fur.

Natural Ice Sculptures

When temperatures plummet at night, smaller waterfalls freeze, only to melt from the warming rays of the sun by day. This alternate freeze-and-thaw rhythm results in bare rock faces becoming decorated with icicle curtains, which cascade down to the flowing river below.

A Playful Fight
As pandas grow up, instead of tumbling over one another in play fights, as they did as young cubs, they will stand up on their hind legs to box. Giant pandas need some support, such as a tree trunk or another panda, to do this, because they cannot walk on their hind legs. So if one panda moves or slips, thereby removing that support, the other inevitably tumbles to the ground.

Walking in the Forest
Pandas walk with a rolling gait with their front feet turned inwards. Despite their size, they move silently on snow-covered ground and in deep snow make tunnels to gain access between one bamboo grove and another. Other animals will then make use of these tunnels.

Paw Print in Snow
Panda tracks are easy to follow after a fresh snowfall.
Researchers use these tracks, as well as radio collars fitted to
some wild pandas, to learn more about how much they move
around and what distance they travel within their territory each day.

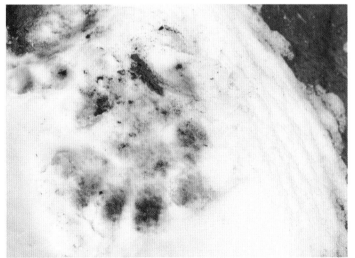

Red Pandas

The red or lesser panda is no match for the giant panda in the worldwide popularity stakes. Nonetheless, it is an enchanting animal that deserves to be better known. Sharing both bear and raccoon characteristics, it has been the subject of much debate as to how it should be classified, but it is now considered to have more affinities with raccoons. In China, red pandas share the same mountain habitats as giant pandas in Sichuan and also occur in neighbouring Yunnan, while a distinct sub-species lives in the Himalayas.

Red Panda in Winter
Red pandas are active all year round and most alert at dawn and dusk. Even after snow has fallen they need to move around to find bamboo. After feeding, they invariably climb back up into a tree for a snooze.

Red Panda Portraits

Red pandas have a foxy face which gives rise to the alternative name of fire fox. The facial markings can vary, but essentially a white area surrounds the dark nose, and a reddish-brown patch runs from the corner of each eye down to the mouth.

On the Ground
Red pandas are capable of moving over the ground at quite different speeds; they can walk at a leisurely pace, trot or run. In each case, the long bushy tail, with its distinctive banding, is carried straight out behind the body. When not in a hurry, a red panda will pause periodically to raise a front paw. In the picture on the right, the retractable claws are clearly visible on one forepaw of a panda which is panting on a warm day.

Up in the Trees

The red panda's lightweight body makes it more agile than the bumbling giant panda and enables it to climb trees more readily. Indeed, a good place to search for red pandas by day is up in the trees. On a sunny day in spring or autumn, they are more likely to be resting out in the open on a horizontal branch. Once they get up and move around they may stand up on a branch, holding on to another with a forepaw as they survey the scene.

Eating Bamboo

Within Wolong, red pandas feed largely on bamboo leaves as well as some shoots. They generally spend time carefully chewing the leaves, which are then digested more efficiently than the giant panda's food. The tip of a bamboo leaf can be seen projecting from the mouth of the panda in the picture below, while the one on the right chews on a stem like a stick of rock, having deftly removed the drier outer covering with its sharp teeth.

Varying the Diet

Just for a change, a red panda
may feed on leaves of herbaceous
plants. Research has shown that
they will eat quite a range of
different plants, including grass
from time to time. Like giant
pandas, they do not hibernate;
in winter they will supplement their
diet by foraging for roots and fruits.

An Arboreal Existence

During the winter, red pandas sleep curled up with their long furry tail wrapped around their body to conserve heat like a duvet, while in summer they flop on to a horizontal branch with their feet hanging down to cool off. They are more omnivorous than giant pandas. In spring they may seek out birds' nests to feast on eggs as well as young chicks which, together with insects, help to add some variety to their 95 per cent bamboo diet.

Grooming

Red pandas regularly groom themselves, after both eating and resting, using their paws to scratch off mud or bits of plants, and their tongue to remove dried mud or even blood after a territorial fight. They do this in a similar way to cats, scratching or licking their fur, with their supple bodies allowing them to reach all parts.

Sniffing a Plant

A red panda sniffs the buds of a plant to check whether it is edible. These pandas also use their sense of smell to detect scent marks left by other pandas within their territory.

Visible Ears

Seen from behind, the reddish-brown ears have obvious pale tips. From the front, they are mostly white with a darker inside. The position of the white fur ensures that from whatever direction it is viewed, a red panda's head shows up against any sombre backdrop.

◀ Sharing a Meal

Young red pandas, before they become territorial, will tolerate sharing the same food source. A moss-covered stone provides a useful elevated support and standing up on their hind legs gains extra height, enabling the paws to reach young bamboo leaves atop the stems. The long bushy tails with their conspicuous banding are clearly visible here.

Standing Up ▶

When a red panda stands on its hind legs for short periods to feed or to survey its surroundings, the base of the tail functions as a third anchor point, like a tripod support. The dark fur can then be seen on the belly and underarms, and inside the legs. Individual variation in facial markings is also apparent here.

Cryptic Colouration

After the green herb layer dies down and reverts to brown leaves and stems, the rich reddish-brown fur blends in quite well with the plant remnants on the forest floor. The white-tipped ears also merge in with snow patches.

Territorial Dispute ▲ ▶

Two pandas fight over their territory in the snow. The fight persisted
for several minutes before one of them fled and raced up a tree.
Only when it paused for breath, turned around and gazed down at
the ground were its blood-stained ears apparent.

◀ Leaving your Mark

Red pandas are highly territorial and both sexes – males
in particular – mark out the boundaries of their patch using
a musky secretion from their anal glands as well as urine
and droppings. If a male encounters a competitor within his
territory and neither gives way by running off, they will fight,
either by rolling on the ground or by standing up on their
hind legs to box with their front paws.

A Passion for Pandas

When I first visited China way back in 1984, I was unable to gain access to see the pandas at Wolong. It was to be over a decade before my dream of seeing my first panda here in Sichuan Province became a reality. When it looked into my eyes, I was captivated by this bumbling bamboo eater. Little did I know that this was to be the start of a prolonged love affair with China's national treasure. Since then, I have devoted more time to photographing this single species than to any other animal anywhere in the world. To date I have made seven trips to China specifically to photograph pandas and this is my third panda book.

The giant panda is the most famous of all China's endemic fauna, but there is a rich assortment of other special animals – not to mention plants – that make this such a biodiverse habitat. So, while a panda

is intent on eating, I spend time making notes of the intricate way it feeds as well as taking habitat shots or looking at the plants and other animals that share its home. Many of the shots portraying varied antics were grabbed in brief moments between bamboo-munching sessions. There was one magical occasion when a curious young captive-bred panda wandered towards me, stood up and grasped a tripod leg. It was far too close for me to even focus a camera, but fortunately someone else was able to capture this precious moment.

Whenever I work with pandas I realize how very fortunate I have been to spend so much time with such a rare animal. I shall forever be lured back to the misty mountains in my endeavour to capture still more intimate moments of the panda's way of life. Human beings are not as well adapted as pandas to walking in deep snow, but with arctic boots and gaiters in winter I never had cold feet.

In recent years a huge amount of time, money and effort have been lavished on conserving the giant panda. We can only hope that this will pay off so that future generations can gain as much pleasure as I have from this unique and quite adorable mammal.

For more panda pictures see:
www.naturalvisions.co.uk – main website
For autographed books, photography tips and hints see:
www.heatherangel.co.uk – Heather's personal website

Acknowledgments

My thanks to the many people who have helped me to capture the panda images: notably Jia Min (gbtlky@mail.sc.cninfo.net), China Span, Joe Van Os Photo Safaris, Zhang Hemin, Director of the China Conservation and Research Center for the Giant Panda, and his staff for assistance with photography at Wolong. Thanks also to the team at David and Charles – Neil Baber, Sarah Clark and Demelza Hookway.

The images in this book were all taken with Nikon cameras – F4 and F5 bodies with film and now D2X bodies for digital capture with a wide range of lenses, from 24mm to 500mm. The 200–400mm f/4 lens is my favourite since it allows for precise in-camera crops. Digital RAW images are backed up in the field on Jobo Giga Vu external hard drives and processed using Adobe CS3 software. Gaining the correct exposure to show detail in both white and black fur can be tricky. I tend to underexpose white areas slightly so that I can fine-tune the exposure on the RAW images. Apart from this, and slight adjustments to the contrast and saturation, none of the images in this book were manipulated.

Further Information

Angel, Heather (2006), *Giant Pandas,* Evans Mitchell Books, ISBN 1-901268-12-8

Schaller, George B. (1993), *The Last Panda,* The University of Chicago Press, ISBN 0-226-73628-8

For information on the work by the World Wide Fund for Nature on giant pandas see:

www.panda.org – click on species, A–Z Index and P to get to giant panda.

Panda cam

Watch pandas feeding and moving around in their spacious enclosures on the panda cam installed at the Smithsonian National Zoological Park in Washington DC, USA. http://nationalzoo.si.edu/Animals/GiantPandas/ – scroll down to see the panda cam.

Mother giant panda with baby statue by Ye Shushan in Chengdu, the capital of Sichuan province where most wild pandas live.